THE LESSON OF ICARUS

retold by Marianne Lenihan
illustrated by Phyllis Pollema Cahill

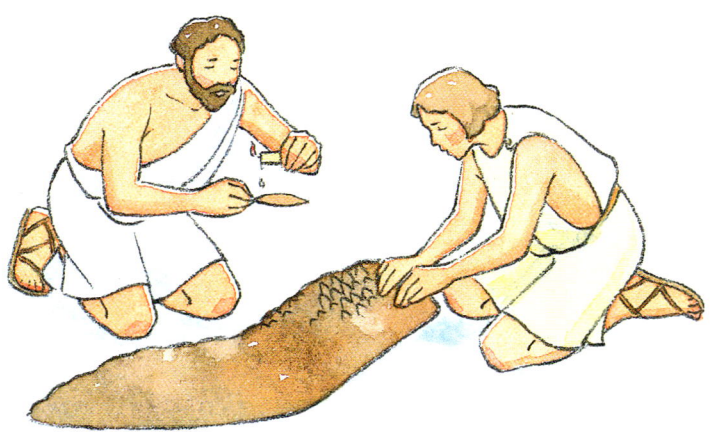

Editorial Offices: Glenview, Illinois • Parsippany, New Jersey • New York, New York
Sales Offices: Needham, Massachusetts • Duluth, Georgia • Glenview, Illinois
Coppell, Texas • Ontario, California • Mesa, Arizona

Every effort has been made to secure permission and provide appropriate credit for photographic material. The publisher deeply regrets any omission and pledges to correct errors called to its attention in subsequent editions.

Unless otherwise acknowledged, all photographs are the property of Scott Foresman, a division of Pearson Education.

Photo locators denoted as follows: Top (T), Center (C), Bottom (B), Left (L), Right (R), Background (Bkgd)

Illustrations by Phyllis Pollema Cahill

ISBN: 0-328-13367-1

Copyright © Pearson Education, Inc.

All Rights Reserved. Printed in the United States of America. This publication is protected by Copyright, and permission should be obtained from the publisher prior to any prohibited reproduction, storage in a retrieval system, or transmission in any form by any means, electronic, mechanical, photocopying, recording, or likewise. For information regarding permission(s), write to: Permissions Department, Scott Foresman, 1900 East Lake Avenue, Glenview, Illinois 60025.

7 8 9 10 V0G1 14 13 12 11 10 09 08

Daedalus was an inventor and a builder. He lived many years ago on the island of Crete.

King Minos asked Daedalus to build a prison for the Minotaur. The Minotaur was part man and part bull.

Daedalus built a maze prison. The Minotaur was trapped in the maze!

Prince Theseus came to Crete soon after. He came to slay the Minotaur and marry the king's daughter. Theseus asked Daedalus for help.

　Daedalus told Theseus to tie one end of a long string to the prison door. He told him to hold the other end until he reached the Minotaur. Then he could follow the trail of string out of the maze.

Theseus killed the Minotaur. Then he asked the princess to marry him.

The princess and Theseus left Crete together. King Minos was angry when he learned that his daughter was gone!

Minos roared, "Daedalus must have helped Theseus! Soldiers, find Daedalus!"
The king's soldiers found Daedalus and his son, Icarus. They locked them both in prison.

"Father, there is no way to get out of this prison," Icarus complained.

Daedalus said, "We'll make wings from feathers and wax. We'll fly out of prison!"

The father and son struggled to make the wings. Finally, they were finished.

The day before the escape, Daedalus warned Icarus, "Do not fly close to the Sun. The wax in your wings will melt. Then you will crash!"

The next day, Daedalus and Icarus flew off the prison tower and into the sky.

"Flying is wonderful!" cried Icarus with a giggle. He was swooping up high and looping down low. But Icarus forgot to pay attention to his father's warning. Suddenly he was drifting too close to the glaring Sun.

    The wax began to melt. His wings came apart. Icarus fell into the sea below and drowned!

    Daedalus landed safely on the island of Sicily. But he was very sad. There, Daedalus built a monument to honor his son Icarus.

What Myths Tell Us

The story of Icarus is a myth. A myth is a tale that has been retold from one generation to another. Myths tell us how some people explained events in nature or tried to teach lessons.

The story of Icarus is one of many famous myths from ancient Greece. Like all ancient Greek myths, it was meant to be told out loud. For many years after the myth was first told, people did not write it down. Because of that, we don't know who first told the myth.

What value or belief does the myth of Icarus express? Why do you think the myth was first told?